BICYCLING AROUND GALENA

A guide to the backroads

Nick Murray (signature)

Nick Murray

Omnivore Press

A division of Nicholas Murray Editorial Services
706 Park Avenue, Galena, Illinois 61036

ISBN: 0-9644209-0-2

Cover photo: Looking west from West Rawlins Road near Elizabeth/Scales Mound Road.

Back cover: The region immediately southeast of Galena, showing the forks off of Blackjack Road. North Irish Hollow goes off to the right; then North Rocky Hill splits off of that to the left. North Pilot Knob branches off to the left from Blackjack. The short, straight road is Deininger Lane, which runs across the north shoulder of Dygert's Mound. (Photo courtesy of the Agricultural Stabilization and Conservation Service, Elizabeth, IL.)

Contents

Preface

Even before part of the annual Cactus Cup bicycle race was held in Galena in the summer of 1994, I was seeing more and more bicycles mounted on the cars and RVs that came into town. I had just started riding the backroads in the region around Galena the summer before on a new mountain bike that would handle the hills and gravel. Riding out into the country was both challenging and exciting, and the more I explored, the more I was drawn by the beautiful secluded hollows and the vistas from the high ridges.

It occurred to me that the people coming here with their bikes would probably appreciate a guide to some of the best places to ride—a guide that would offer more information than a map can give about the terrain and condition of the roads. I started recording the routes I was riding and talking with people about what I was doing, and found a lot of enthusiasm for the idea of such a book.

Riding by cemeteries in the country and seeing piles of old mine tailings keeps the region's history in mind, and so these descriptions include some historical notes and a few old photographs as well. It deepens my feeling for the land to know, for instance, that many of the roads in the area began as stage routes connecting the little settlements that lay between what are now the major towns, or as wagon tracks that converged on grist mills or smelting furnaces.

So here it is, a guide to the backroads in roughly a 15-mile radius around Galena that sweeps from the north to the east and south, with maps, photographs, and a little historical flavoring. I hope it leads you to as much pleasure as I've had riding these hills and valleys.

Will the Freeway Come?

If you're interested in preserving the natural beauty of many of these routes, you should be aware that the Illinois Department of Transportation (IDOT) is planning a major four-lane freeway between Freeport and Galena that will run through either Long Hollow or Irish Hollow, run northwest toward Galena on the eastern side of existing U.S. 20, and then cut through the valley northeast of Horseshoe Mound, looping through the area northeast of town to meet Highway 20 at the junction with Route 84 north of Galena. To stay abreast of current developments, and to find out how to express your views on this project, call the IDOT planning and study group at 1-800-837-RT20.

IDOT seems committed to the project, although District Engineer William D. Ost has said that the Advisory Council will look at the "no-build" option. "If you feel a new highway is not needed," he said, "you should tell IDOT and your elected representatives, and your input will make a difference." If you are committed to the no-build option, you may want to get in touch with the Freeway Watch Committee, an alternative study group whose position is that current and projected problems with U.S. 20 can be adequately and more economically resolved by a carefully considered and thorough upgrading of the existing road, with appropriate bypasses around the towns that suffer from so much through traffic. You can get on their mailing list by writing to the Freeway Watch Committee, P.O. Box 339, Elizabeth, Illinois, 61028.

Acknowledgments

Throughout the writing of this guide, I've had the encouragement and help of many friends. For sharing their historical knowledge of the region, I want to thank H. Scott Wolf, of the Alfred Mueller Historical Collection at the Galena Public Library; Daryl Watson, of the Galena Historical Society; and especially Dick Vincent of Galena, who was kind enough to share his stories and his immense collection of photographs with me.

The maps were done by Tom Leveque, although I must take responsibility for the labeling of the roads (and any mislabeling, or just plain lack of labeling).

The aerial photograph on the back cover was made available through the courtesy of the Agricultural Stabilization & Conservation Service in Elizabeth. Many thanks to Cory Cassens, Sheila Sadler, and Mildred Allendorf, whose patient efforts helped me find what I needed.

For his skillful and timely help with shooting copy negatives, developing, and printing, my thanks go to George Bookless of Galena. The photos of old mines and smelting furnaces are from the Historical Collection of the Galena Public Library, located with alacrity by H. Scott Wolf. All the other photographs are mine. George produced the final prints for all black-and-white shots except the last three, which were done by Wm. C. Brown Communications from my color slides.

My thanks are due as well to Dave Connolly, of Galena's Cover to Cover bookstore. Dave's encouragement and suggestions regarding marketing and distribution have been invaluable.

For the cover design and for their fruitful comments on the title, I'm grateful to the talented people at the Creative Department in Galena: Jim Carlson, Amy Albright, and especially John Albright, who did the stat work on the maps and laid out the front cover.

Special thanks also to Sara Fisher, who gave the page proofs a final reading before they went to the printer. Her careful eye caught quite a few things that had eluded me. As they say in publishing, "To typo is human; to proof, divine." On my head be any errors that remain.

The book was printed at Wm. C. Brown Communications, and I want to thank Dan Nichols for the time and attention he gave to getting this project under way when his desk was laden with bigger fish to fry.

Finally, I'm grateful to my wife, Jo, and daughter, Erin, for their encouragement, patience, and good humor while I disappeared during the day for "road research" and holed up in the evenings to write. Jo also designed and produced, with Erin's help, the display stands. And thanks again, Jo, for giving me the wheels that got me started on this project and carried me through to its completion.

Introduction

The countryside around Galena is some of the most beautiful in the Midwest, but it is definitely hilly, and many of the nicest roads to ride are unsurfaced, so a mountain bike is best. If you're riding a road bike, you'll need low gearing and reinforced tires with some tread if you want to spend much time on the unsurfaced roads. Some people here ride them on road bikes, but they have years and miles of biking under their belts. If you have no experience in controlling a road bike on dirt and gravel, plan to stay on surfaced roads. The maps done for this book indicate unsurfaced roads by white stippling. Jo Daviess County roads are always subject to improvement, however, so be aware that what were unsurfaced roads when I was writing this may have been partially or completely surfaced by the time you ride them.

So far, there are no designated bike trails in Jo Daviess County; Illinois lags far behind its neighbors in accommodating bicycle transportation. A group is at work here, however, that hopes to get some trails developed on the area's old railroad beds. For information on their current plans, and to find out how to make a donation (they are a not-for-profit corporation), write to the Jo Daviess Scenic Trails Corporation, P.O. Box 284, Galena, Illinois, 61036.

Looking west from the east end of West Miner Road

These descriptions don't include any off-road biking, but you can check with Chestnut Mountain Resort for information on their off-road trails (815-777-1320). Several of the routes I describe, however, include stretches on unsurfaced roads that are quite secluded (for example, Posey Hollow, Bowden Road, Girot Hill Road, and Diggin Hill Road), and you can certainly get the feeling of being deep in the country, if not actually off the road.

Please remember to be considerate of people's privacy. Respect closed gates on farm roads, and be aware that many a side lane off these back roads, though it may run for a mile or so, is going to bring you into someone's yard. They may have a very territorial dog. They may be doing some coed naked tractor repair. There's a fair chance they won't appreciate an intrusion—but if you have a problem, most will be glad to help.

Safety

All the routes described are over working county roads; you ride them at your own risk. Stay alert for traffic, including farm vehicles coming out from fields, and remember that cows and hogs sometimes get out onto the roads. Be aware that because traffic is light on most of these roads, many drivers figure they aren't going to meet anyone coming around the next curve, or they may start pretending they're at the Grand Prix. Stay well to the right, *especially* going up and down hills and around curves. If you're working too hard on an uphill to have good control of your bike, go for safety first—swallow your pride and walk it for a while.

Be sure your brakes are in good working order. Don't fly downhill. If you just can't follow that advice, at least don't ignore it unless there are no farm lanes or driveways ahead, no traffic ahead or behind, and you can see to the bottom of the grade. *Never* turn it loose downhill where curves keep you from seeing what's ahead, and always be alert for loose gravel on curves. Rain will sometimes wash large patches of it across surfaced roads.

Drivers

If you are driving rather than bicycling on these backroads, I encourage you to stay on the surfaced roads. One reason is safety: it's extremely easy to start sliding and lose control on gravel, and sharp curves have a way of coming up suddenly over the crest of a hill. These roads are not meant for speed, and the curves are often quite tight. The roads are also narrow, with barely enough (and sometimes not enough) room for two vehicles to get by each other.

Another reason is that you probably won't like what traveling these roads does to your car. Gravel thrown by your own tires or passing pickup trucks chips paint, "washboard" sections going uphill rattle your shocks and teeth, and dust and grit get into everything. People who live along these roads dislike the dust settling on porches and coming in windows, so the less raised, the better.

One road in particular to avoid is South River Road, which is not passable by car south of the base of Chestnut Mountain.

Regional History

Geology

Galena lies in the heart of what is known as the Driftless Area, a region near the southern limit of glacial expansion during the last Ice Age that the glaciers bypassed, leaving it unaffected by the scouring of glacial movement and the massive deposits of soil that tended to level the land from which the glaciers retreated. The mineral wealth of the Driftless Area was thus left exposed at the surface instead of buried, and the surrounding topography is ancient, shaped only by the work of water and wind.

As you study the landscape from the roads on the ridge crests, it's easy to get a feeling for how it has been shaped. There is a basically level horizon at 800 to 900 feet, broken by the mounds and higher ridges that rise to more than 1100 feet. (Charles Mound, northeast of Scales Mound, is the highest point in Illinois, rising over 1200 feet.) At the end of the last Ice Age, increasing rainfall and glacial meltwater cut the large-scale features of the landscape, leaving the mounds and ridges. The ridge that carries Stagecoach Trail from just west of Scales Mound to just west of North Ford Road is a good example, cut by the waters of what has now become the East Fork of the Galena River (you'll climb this ridge if you ride the Ford Road Loop).

All this water turned the ancient Mississippi into a wide torrent that cut its bed down more than 100 feet, forming the bluffs along its banks. The tributary rivers and streams then cut their valleys deeper near the Mississippi. With time, the big river slowed, narrowed, and filled with silt, so that its waters rose and backed up into rivers like the Galena, making them sluggish and prone to fill with silt in their turn.

The Mississippi is currently at an elevation of just under 600 feet, and the land around it has been cut into a maze of hills and valleys by the rivers and streams that ultimately find their way to it. Away from the Mississippi, most of the stream beds you'll cross or ride along are at around 700 feet. The Galena River is at about 600 feet and rises quite gradually; it doesn't reach 700 feet until the area near Buncombe Road, on the way to New Diggings in Wisconsin. When you ride these hills, then, you can expect to be rising and falling anywhere from 100 to 200 feet on the longest hills.

The Galena History Museum

There's no better way to get a feeling for the dramatic topography of the region than to visit the museum of the Galena Historical Society on Bench Street and spend some time looking at the large, three-dimensional model created by Richard Tickner. You'll enjoy the rest of the museum, too. I encourage you to spend an hour or two there before riding into the country.

Mines

I've mentioned the locations of old mining sites, smelting furnaces, and mills at several points to give a feeling for the history of the country you'll be riding through. Since people often skip the acknowledgments in the Preface to a book, I want to say again here that I'm grateful to H. Scott Wolf, of the Galena Library's Historical Collection; Dick Vincent, who has spent 40 years traveling through this region and collecting photographs and stories; and Daryl Watson, of the Galena Historical Society, for taking time to share this information with me.

Do not venture into any mines you may find.

Pockets of "dead air," which contains no oxygen and can kill in a few minutes, may exist in the shafts. Some people have gone into these mines, but as Dick Vincent (who told me of several people who lost their lives) says, "They're fortunate. God didn't want 'em, and the Devil knew he'd get 'em sooner or later."

The State of Illinois is currently inspecting and sealing many old mine shafts in the region, but many of them are still open, and several are visible from the routes described. If you are tempted to ignore gates and fences, and decide to trespass in order to hike around in some of these locations (I'm not suggesting this—only acknowledging human nature), stay alert and keep your eyes on the ground around you. Many ventilation shafts, vertical and deep, dot the hills, and they are often obscured by brush.

Riding Out

These cautions given, I'll say again that riding around the Galena region in Jo Daviess County will take you through some truly beautiful country and provide hours of great exercise. The routes described vary in length and difficulty, and with the help of the maps included, you can plan many variations on the loops I've suggested. I have tried always, however, to choose the safest and most scenic routes. Occasionally, I'll describe alternatives, and you'll find separate notes on many roads not included in the routes planned.

The maps overlap each other, so that it's easy to get oriented as you move from one to another. I haven't included a map of Galena itself, but there's a good one (Galena/Jo Daviess County) available at the Chamber of Commerce (in the old railroad depot at the foot of Bouthillier on the east side of the river). It will come in handy for finding your way easily out of town, and you can use it for exploring the town. Galena's neighborhoods are a worthwhile tour in themselves, and offer a variety of beautiful views and secluded surprises. (Check out Hickory Street or Division Street, for instance, between Washington and Ridge.)

I'll refer to the following three exits from Galena in all the routes that are described. As a common reference point for starting out, I've used the main intersection of Highway 20 and Riverside Drive (Main Street), which I'll call the *river intersection*.

Northeast

Ride down Main Street across Franklin and Meeker, and out Dewey to the junction of West Buckhill and North Council Hill. You're following the same route taken by the main trail of the Frink & Walker Stage Line out of Galena in the days before the Illinois Central railroad came through. To your left at that junction was the location of Hughlett's Furnace, a large smelting operation, and on the hill between Buckhill and Council Hill were the Buck and Doe Mines, "where it all started" for the mining industry in Galena. The mines were named for the Indian "buck" who owned them and the women ("does") who did most of the work. The Indians traded lead to the early settlers, until they started making their own strikes.

Southeast

Ride over the river southeast on Highway 20, turn right on Third Street, and then left on Rives Street one block to Blackjack Road.

Hughlett's Furnace

Northwest

From Main Street, cross Highway 20 at the lights, continuing past what some folks call the Kentucky Fried Professional Building (on your left), and turn right up Gear Street (you'll want your lowest range).

Routes to Avoid Out of Galena

Highway 20   Avoid leaving Galena on Highway 20 in either direction. There's no good reason to ride out southeast. If you've just got to get to Happy Joe's (or maybe you're staying at the Best Western, next door), avoid the highway going up from the river intersection by turning left on Park Avenue, just over the bridge, and right on Bouthillier. A steep but short climb takes you past Grant's home, and on to the highway. If you want to get out to the Galena Territory, there's a way in from the north, off of Stagecoach Trail, which I'll describe later.

If you insist on riding Highway 20 northwest, toward Dubuque, bypass the section that leads up from the river intersection, where there are lots of trucks and almost no shoulder. To connect with Highway 20 heading northwest, you have two main options:

- **Gear Street:** From the river intersection, cross Highway 20 and take South Bench Street past the Kentucky Fried Professional Building. Take the first right, get into your lowest gear, and follow Gear Street up to where it hits the highway, near McDonald's.

- **Franklin Street:** Ride down Main Street to the stop sign, and turn left on Franklin. About halfway up, when you see Dillon's Tavern on your right at Division Street, move to the left side of the road and get on the sidewalk to stay out of traffic. Staying on the road isn't as bad as it was, though, now that it's been resurfaced and widened. Riding up Franklin brings you to Highway 20 near the Galena water tower.

Stagecoach Trail Stagecoach Trail, which leads east out of Galena from Recreation Park, is heavily traveled, but not quite as dangerous as Highway 20, because there are seldom large trucks, and there's usually some shoulder to the road. There are certainly some beautiful stretches on Stagecoach. People drive fast, though, and curves and hills decrease visibility, so I generally advise you to avoid it. For some loops, however, Stagecoach is clearly the most efficient route; just stay especially alert if you ride it.

The distances and times indicated for all these routes are approximate, and all times are round-trip times (actual time in the saddle—not counting stops to enjoy the view). All distances are measured from the river intersection at the Highway 20 bridge over the Galena River. I figured an average of 8 mph, but you'll make better time on some of the routes with fewer hills, or if you want to ride at more than a leisurely pace.

West, Northwest, and North

Introduction

The region directly west of Galena doesn't offer as many good opportunities for bicycling as you'll find in other directions. The West Cross/Red Gates Loop is the only one described in that direction. It is close and easy to navigate, so I have not shown it on the accompanying map (Map 1). Check the Map/Guide to Galena and Jo Daviess County distributed by the Chamber of Commerce (in the old railroad depot off of Park Avenue) to help you find your way—you'll want a copy of this map anyway for general use. The Red Gates Spur off of this loop brings you close to the Mississippi, and it's a very pleasant ride. (Ferry Landing Road, of course, also goes down to the river, but I don't recommend riding it, as explained in the Notes.) To the northwest and north, however, there are some very interesting roads to travel. The trip to Sinsinawa Mound offers sweeping views of the region, and you can actually get into an old lead mine up in Vinegar Hill.

West Cross / Red Gates Loop

Time: 3/4 hour   **Distance:** 5.9 miles   **Conditions:** All surfaced

This is a nice, relatively short ride that's great when you don't have a lot of time. It provides a good workout and some beautiful scenery, with an optional spur towards the Mississippi (it dead-ends at the Illinois Central tracks along the river) that adds 2.2 miles and about a half-hour to the ride.

The area you'll ride through was known as the West Diggings, and was heavily mined, especially south of West Cross Road. One of Galena's most prominent early settlers, Hezekiah Gear (for whom Gear Street is named), made one of his major strikes there. Riding west on West Cross, look to your left down the creek at the bottom of the first downhill, and you can still see part of an old building on the site of the Merry Widow and Tenstrike mines.

Tramway for the Merry Widow and Tenstrike mines

The Route

Take the northwest way out, and ride up Gear Street to the intersection with Ferry Landing Road. Turn left, and just past the bottom of the steep downhill, go right on West Cross Road. An early settler, Owen Reilly, had his home here, and news of gatherings in "Reilly's Grove" appears in old issues of the Galena newspaper. There's a nice hollow, and a couple of hills, and then West Cross bends 90 degrees to the right and downhill. To your left as you make this turn was the West Diggings schoolhouse. The downhill steepens just before the intersection with West Red Gates Road, and you can't see traffic, so don't fly down it—use your brakes, and watch for loose gravel on the road.

To finish the loop, bend right, and take Red Gates to Highway 20. Turn right at the highway, and stay right to get back on Gear Street, within sight just a short distance away. You'll go by Ferry Landing again, and then have a good coast down Gear back to the river intersection. Get on the brakes early for the stop sign at the bottom of Gear.

Red Gates Spur

A beautiful addition to this ride is to go left at the intersection with Red Gates and ride through the hollow down to the railroad tracks. On the bluffs that overlook the river are many Indian burial sites. Early settlers came here to cut wood for fuel and construction.

When the weeds aren't too high, you can see how to get under the tracks just to your left at the dead end. If you want to get to the river, you can go under this bridge and a short way through the woods, which are open enough to ride in if the ground is dry. (Depending on the river level, it can be a mud swamp.) Ride back and finish the loop as explained above.

Notes

Ferry Landing Road   Ferry Landing Road leads down to the Mississippi and dead-ends at a small marina. I don't recommend riding it, because the traffic is sometimes crazy, and it's a major workout, both going and coming back. The gravel shoulder on the hills is washed out in many places. If you decide to ride it, keep a sharp eye out for traffic behind you, and be ready to dismount and get off the road if you happen to be where two cars are going to pass in opposite directions.

Just before you go right off of Ferry Landing onto West Cross, you'll see a road going off to the left. This is a dead-end road that leads into a new residential development. It's a nice spur to add to this ride—good views once you're up the hill.

North Cross Road   Not too far before West Cross bends right and downhill to meet Red Gates, you'll see North Cross Road (unsurfaced) going off to your left. This soon becomes a private road, leading to farms. The same is true of its other branch, which continues straight where West Cross goes right and downhill. Please be considerate of these people's privacy—you'll just wind up at someone's barn or front yard.

Sinsinawa Mound Loop

Time: 3 hours   **Distance:** 24 miles   **Conditions:** All surfaced

Sinsinawa Mound, home of the Sinsinawa Dominican Sisters, is an interesting place to visit, and makes an especially nice early morning trip. You can walk up a trail to the top of the mound, if you want a little more exercise, and the Dominican Center is a beautiful place to spend some time.

If you call a day or so ahead (608-748-4411), you may be able to arrange a group tour. Otherwise, for people dropping in, access to the buildings is limited. You're welcome to walk the grounds and visit the chapel on the top floor of the round building, as well as the bookstore.

The earliest settler here, George Wallace Jones, built a log cabin at the Mound in 1828 and had a smelting operation. The stone granary that he built still stands among the buildings of the Dominican Center. It also served as a sheltering fort during the time of the Black Hawk War. Jones was a friend of Jefferson Davis, who visited him there several times. He also became a friend of Father Samuel Mazzuchelli, to whom he finally sold Sinsinawa Mound. A priest of great energy and architectural skill, Father Mazzuchelli founded the Dominican Center there, as well as many churches in the area.

The time and distance I've given are for what I think is the nicest (not the shortest) route, involving the least distance on a major road. I'll describe some options in the Notes.

Stone granary at Sinsinawa Mound, built in 1832

The Route

Take the northeast route out of Galena. At the intersection of Council Hill and Buckhill, bear left on North Council Hill Road. About 2 miles up, go left on West Council Hill Road, which takes you west to Route 84. Go left again, and ride south for almost a mile; then go right on High Ridge Road. Traffic on Route 84 is fast and sometimes heavy, but you're not on it for long, and the shoulder is generally good.

A little more than 2 miles up High Ridge, you'll come to a three-way fork. Take the middle road, following High Ridge uphill. Bending left on West Valley Road would bring you to Menominee Road; bending right on West Valley would loop you back to Route 84, about 2 miles north of where you got on it from West Council Hill.

About 2 more miles along High Ridge, make a left on Sinsinawa Road. For about 0.2 mile, you're headed due west right on the Illinois/Wisconsin border, and then the road bends northwest into Grant County and on to Sinsinawa, at the intersection with County Z.

To return, ride back the way you came.

Portage

Another possibility, which would shorten the round trip by about 6 miles, is to load your bike on the car and drive north to the intersection of Route 84 and Highway 20, where the highway bends left by Fran's Cafe. Leave the car in the little roadside park there, and ride about 0.3 mile up Route 84 to High Ridge Road. Follow the main route described from there.

Extension to Hazel Green

If you're up for a slightly longer (28.6 miles) ride with a break for food and drink, you can ride from the Mound over to the town of Hazel Green. You could continue north on County Z to Highway 11 and turn right for a 6.3-mile, half-hour ride to Hazel Green, but that's a major road, and you'll have trucks going by at a good clip, as well as other fast traffic. I recommend a slightly longer, safer, and more scenic route (7.4 miles, all surfaced; about 40 minutes).

Go back the way you came, down Sinsinawa Road, and when you come to North High Ridge, cross it, continuing east on Sinsinawa. There's a mild downhill into the Sinsinawa River Valley, and after about a mile in the valley the road makes a long, generally gradual climb to meet Route 84, where you turn left and ride north into Hazel Green (about 1.3 miles to the heart of town). You can get breakfast at the Long Branch tavern.

You can return to Galena by riding south on Route 84, but stay alert. It's a main road with fast traffic, but you won't see many large trucks. There's a decent shoulder, and visibility is generally good. Don't take it all the way in to the intersection with Highway 20, though. Go left on West Council Hill, and right on North Council Hill, heading back into Galena the way you came out on the route described first (the distance along this return is 9.2 miles from Hazel Green). You can go left sooner off Route 84 at West Furlong, but then you either have to be ready for the strenuous ride on hilly North Meridian, or go on east to North Birkbeck in order to get back to Council Hill. If you do the latter, you

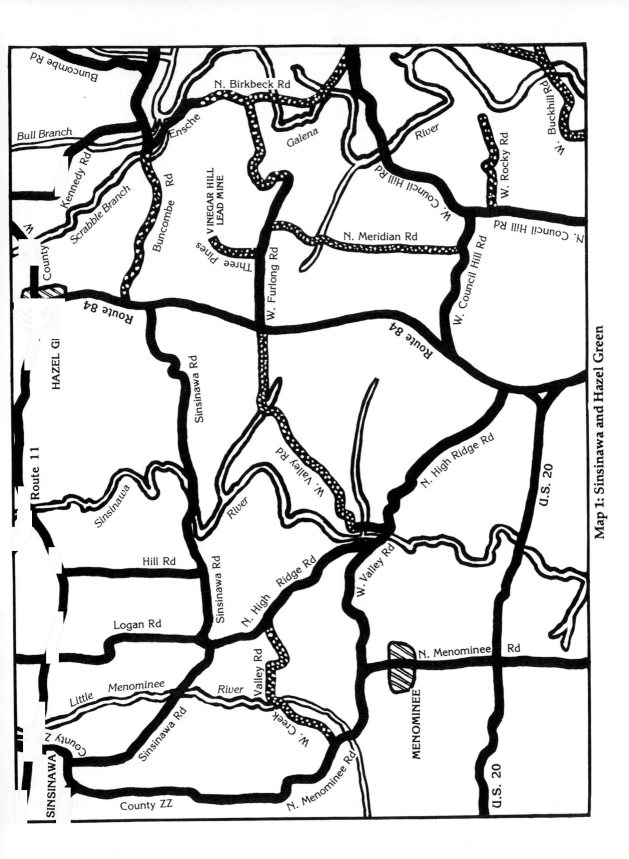

Map 1: Sinsinawa and Hazel Green

might as well go the whole nine yards and choose the following option for your return.

Buncombe Road Return   If you took enough time in Hazel Green to get a good rest from the saddle, and you'd like to extend your ride on the way back, you can avoid most of Route 84 by looping out east on Buncombe Road (first left after leaving Hazel Green going south on Route 84; unsurfaced on this section). Buncombe takes you into an area where there was intense mining activity, which I'll say a little more about in the next section on routes to the northeast.

If you're interested in geology, Buncombe Road offers a good opportunity to see the rock stratum that contained most of the lead deposits in the region. Known as "Galena dolomite," it is an Ordovician dolomite characterized by shiny white chunks of chert. Look on the north side in the road cut as you approach the Galena River, and especially in the bluff at the northeast corner of the junction of Buncombe and Kennedy Road, which comes down from the north just past Ensche Road. An excellent short book describing a geological tour of the area is available in the Historical Collection of the Galena Library: *Guide to the Geology of the Galena Area,* by David Reinertsen (published by the Illinois State Geological Survey, Natural Resources Bldg., 615 E. Peabody Drive, Champaign, IL, 61820).

You'll cross the Scrabble Branch of the Galena River and pass the site of the old Buncombe School to your right on the flat just before Ensche Road. Turn right on Ensche (surfaced) at the Galena River, and before long you'll be doing some uphill work past a major show of mine tailings on your right. Follow Ensche south into Illinois, where it becomes North Birkbeck Road (unsurfaced). The tailings you'll see down in the pasture hollow to your right as you approach West Furlong are the only sign left of the old Northwestern Mine. Go on by the junction with West Furlong, and stay on Birkbeck to West Council Hill Road. Turn right, and follow Council Hill back to Galena (10.8 miles from where you leave Route 84 to the river intersection in Galena).

Menominee Route

Another route to Sinsinawa that avoids all but a very short stretch on Highway 20 is to ride out of Galena up Franklin Street, and then continue up Highway 20 for about a half mile to Chetlain Lane, at the Microswitch Plant. Go left on Chetlain, and follow it west to Menominee Road, where you turn right, heading

The Northwestern Mine on North Birkbeck Road

north. (Chetlain is a rollercoaster, though, and you may not want to work this hard at the beginning of a relatively long ride.)

Menominee Road takes you all the way up to Sinsinawa. You'll cross Highway 20 and go on through the little town of Menominee, which has a tavern/general store (not open until 2:00 P.M.). Menominee Road becomes County ZZ once you enter Wisconsin, and meets County Z at the Mound. High Ridge Road and the main building of the Center are to your right at that point. This route is not quite as pleasant or scenic; traffic is heavier and faster, and the country is generally more open and not quite as hilly. The distance is about the same (maybe 0.3 mile shorter).

Note on Map 1 that from the High Ridge route, you also have the option of bending left on West Valley Road at the three-way intersection, which brings you west to Menominee Road about a mile before the village of Menominee. Just continue west on Menominee as you meet it.

Vinegar Hill Loop (Vinegar Hill Lead Mine)

Time: 2 1/2 hours   **Distance:** 15.9 miles

Conditions: 4.7 miles unsurfaced: 2.5 miles on North Birkbeck Road, and 2.2 miles on North Meridian Road. Meridian is a rollercoaster, but it's nice country and worth the workout.

This is more strenuous than the Council Hill/Buckhill Loop (see next section), but it's a beautiful ride, and also offers the opportunity to visit the only lead mine in Illinois that's open for tours—the Vinegar Hill Lead Mine and Museum, which has been in the Furlong family since 1818. You can bring a sack lunch, and enjoy a break about halfway through the loop. The tour lasts about a half-hour, and costs $4.00 per person ($2.00 for students).

The region along this route is rich in mining history, and tailings are visible at many points. The introduction to the next section includes historical notes about the area around the junction of Council Hill and Buckhill Roads. So many routes pass through here that I've given the information there to avoid repeating it.

The Route

Take the northeast way out of town, and follow North Council Hill Road out through Millbrig Hollow, where it crosses the Galena River. Down the farm road to your right, which follows an old railroad grade, there was a large mill. Just past the Grant Hill Cemetery after you climb up from the hollow, turn left on North Birkbeck Road, which takes you back down into the Galena River Valley. The well-kept farmhouse that you'll see to your right after you cross the river was built in 1870 by a wealthy landowner and riverboat gambler, who eventually lost everything. The house was abandoned for a long time before being restored. The wife of the present owner is from the Birkbeck family.

Just past this house, turn left on West Furlong Road, and you'll see the remains of a root cellar—the only sign left of a house that used to stand here 100 years ago. West Furlong runs east through a small creek valley, and then swings south and up to the ridge, where Furlong (now surfaced) continues to your right. After about a half-mile, North Meridian Road takes off to your left. Years ago, this junction was the site of a general store and a church. If you're going to tour the Vinegar Hill Lead Mine, go on past Meridian about 0.3 mile, and turn right on Three Pines Road, which leads to a pleasant picnic area and the start of the mine tour.

The entry area to the Vinegar Hill Lead Mine

To return to Galena, take North Meridian Road, which runs almost straight south along the Fourth Principal Meridian, a major reference point for surveyors. You'll pass close to what was the last working mine in the area, the Eagle Picher Mine, on the third uphill of this rolling road. One more down-and-up and you hit West Council Hill Road. The area northeast of this intersection was the site of Hezekiah Gear's first big strike—the one Jim Post sings about in *Galena Rose* (see it if you haven't)—and here he had his smelting operation, Gear's Furnace. Go left on West Council Hill, and shortly you'll hit North Council Hill, where you turn right and head back into Galena the way you came out.

Notes

Meridian Bypass   If you want to avoid the rollercoaster ride on North Meridian Road, you can take West Furlong straight west to Route 84, turn left, and go south to West Council Hill, where you turn left again and go to North Council Hill, turning right to head back into Galena. That stretch of Route 84 is pretty much straight and level, so visibility is good. Still, it's a major road; traffic is usually fast and can be heavy, so be alert. This adds 4.1 miles to the loop (all easy riding on surfaced roads). Don't follow Route 84 down to the junction with Highway 20 as a way back to Galena; go for the lowest risk level and the most pleasant ride.

West Valley Road   If you would like to see one of the most beautiful little valleys in the region and don't mind adding 6.8 miles (2.4 unsurfaced) to this loop, take West Furlong to Route 84, as you would to bypass Meridian, and then go straight across Route 84 onto West Valley Road. For a couple of miles the road rolls through pastureland and cornfields, and then drops into the Sinsinawa River Valley, where another valley formed by a branch creek comes in from the east. The road becomes surfaced here, and you cross the Sinsinawa River and ride south along a low limestone bluff and on to the three-way junction with North High Ridge Road. Bear left after the stop sign to get on North High Ridge, and follow it up to Route 84, where you turn left and go up 0.8 mile to West Council Hill. Turn right there, and then right again on North Council Hill and back to Galena.

Northeast

Introduction

The area bounded by North and West Council Hill Roads, West Stagecoach Trail, and North Ford/North Hill Roads offers a variety of loops. I'll describe a few nice ones, and you can string together your own variations and combinations with the help of the maps. Maps 2 and 3 overlap quite a bit for convenience; Map 2 shows more to the east and south, and Map 3 shows more to the west and north. Some interesting historical sites are in this region, and since several loops take you past the same points, I'll talk about them here, rather than repeat the information in each route description.

South of the junction of Buckhill and Bowden Roads, where the East Fork of the Galena River joins the main channel, stood Bowden's Furnace, one of many smelting furnaces in the area. Nothing is left of it now; you'll see a house standing on the site. There were more than 20 furnaces in the region, and each of them burned four to eight cords of wood a day, which is the main reason for the barren hillsides you see in old photos of Galena.

At Council Hill in 1832, Henry Gratiot, the Indian agent from Galena, met with Chief Black Hawk and persuaded him not to attack Galena. Council Hill was the first stop on the main stage route out of Galena, from the 1830s until the 1850s.

The Council Hill House, a large old inn, was off to the right, just before North Hill Road, and on the left coming into town was the Mayne House, a two-story building that had a general store and barber shop. The building is still there, just beyond the white town hall, also on your left as you're coming from Galena. The stone part that you see first is part of the original building.

Council Hill Station was built when the Illinois Central railroad came through in 1854, putting an end to the Frink & Walker Stage Line. There was a mill and a large stockyard here in those days. If you stop here to rest and talk, you'll probably hear some stories about the old times.

Miners migrated up the Galena River Valley in search of new strikes, and rich deposits were found just north of the Illinois line, especially in the area of Buncombe and Kennedy Roads, and up at New Diggings. Up Kennedy Road, just beyond where you cross the Bull Branch heading north, the entrance to the Kennedy Mine is still visible to your left. The Chicago & Northwestern railroad had a station near the junction of Buncombe and North Roads at the Galena River. When the foliage is off the trees, you can see an old tunnel through the bluff if you stand on Buncombe Road at that junction and look south and just a little west. More about New Diggings appears in the introduction to that route.

By the way, in Wisconsin, the Galena River is known as the Fever River, even though (to avoid confusion) I'll consistently refer to it as the Galena River, and have labeled it that way on the map. But if you've come up from Illinois and are having breakfast in Hazel Green, you'll get on better with the morning euchre players if you call it the Fever River.

Council Hill / Buckhill Loop

Time: 1 3/4 hours   **Distance:** 15.4 miles

Conditions: 3.5 miles unsurfaced on North Bowden Road and on Buckhill on the flat along the Galena River. There's a nice downhill into Millbrig Hollow, and then a long and sometimes steep uphill, and one steep climb up Buckhill on your way back, just as it becomes surfaced.

This is a relatively easy loop that gives you a good look at the variety in the countryside northeast of Galena. In the Galena River Valley on Buckhill, you'll pass the site of the old Bowden's Furnace.

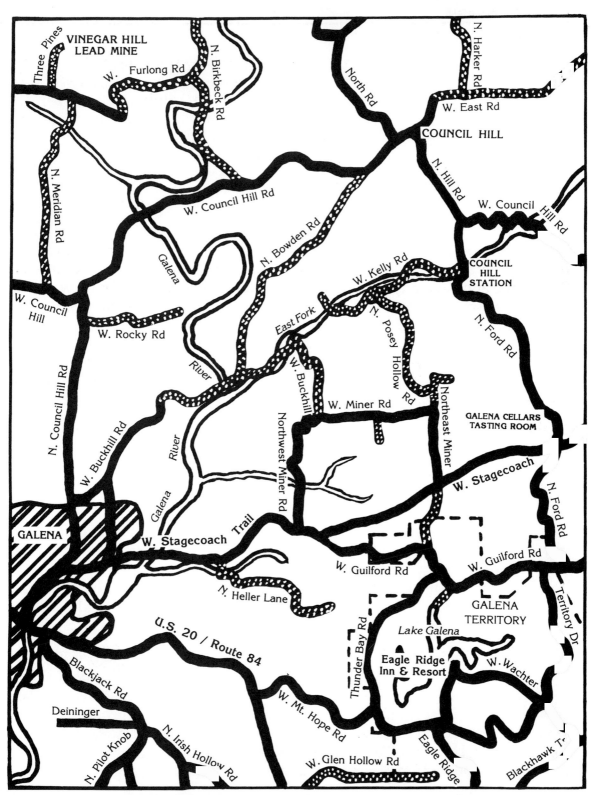

Map 2: Vinegar Hill, Council Hill, Posey Hollow, Ford Road

The Galena River from the bridge at Millbrig Hollow

The Route

Take the northeast way out of town, and follow North Council Hill Road down into Millbrig Hollow. You'll cross the Galena River and then ride uphill past Grant Hill Cemetery and past Birkbeck Road on your left. Go on to North Bowden Road, turn right, and follow it down to West Buckhill Road. At that intersection stood Bowden's Furnace. There is a house there now, and hardly a sign left of this major smelting operation.

Turning right on Buckhill, you'll cross the Galena River again, and ride about a half-mile in the valley before the road becomes surfaced and heads uphill along a wooded ravine. The second house on your right was an old schoolhouse. Follow Buckhill past the junction with School Section Road (which leads down to West Stagecoach at Recreation Park on the east edge of Galena) and back to North Council Hill. Be ready for the stop sign at the end of the downhill leading to the intersection. From here, it's back into town the way you came out.

Bowden's Furnace stood at Buckhill and Bowden Roads

Note

West Rocky Road   If you've got some energy to spare, riding down Rocky Road to the Galena River Valley is a nice side trip along a wooded hillside. The road dead-ends at a riverside farm, however, so you've got to ride back up what you came down—in the 1.1 miles up to Council Hill, the road rises 230 feet. Most of it is gradual, but there's a short stretch of 11% grade just before you get back up to Council Hill Road.

Across the river from here was Tuttle's Mill, and there is an old railroad grade along the river going north to Millbrig Hollow and beyond (you can see part of it from Birkbeck Road if you ride the Vinegar Hill Loop or the return described for the New Diggings Loop; it goes off to your right as you cross the Galena River). Perhaps someday there will be bicycle trails along some of these old railroad beds, but for now the only way to see places like the old Tuttle's Mill is by canoe.

The view from West Miner Road, looking east

Posey Hollow / Council Hill Loop

Time: 2 1/2 hours   **Distance:** 20.2 miles

Conditions: 4.7 miles unsurfaced; 2.3 miles on Buckhill, and 2.4 miles on Posey Hollow Road.

This loop gives you some nice views of the surrounding country from West Miner Road, and then Posey Hollow Road takes you on a long, gentle descent through a wooded hollow and under the Illinois Central tracks through a short tunnel underpass. There's an old iron bridge on Kelly Road, which runs through the valley formed by the East Fork of the Galena River. On the way in to Council Hill, you'll have a chance to rest and get a cold drink from Tom Bruun's little store at Council Hill Station before going up to West Council Hill Road. There used to be a stockyard here, and down behind the store was a mill.

The Route

Take the northeast way out of town, and go up West Buckhill Road. Follow it out along the ridge and down into the Galena River Valley. You'll cross the river just before the intersection with Bowden Road. Stay on Buckhill, which will bend south and up to West Miner Road (surfaced). Turn left on West Miner and follow it to its end at Northeast Miner Road, where you turn left. A short way north, you'll bend left and be on North Posey Hollow Road—there's no sign. (Going straight would take you into a private farm lane.)

It's a beautiful ride down Posey Hollow. After you go through the short tunnel under the Illinois Central tracks, turn right on West Kelly Road. (Going left would bring you to a private home, the old Abley house—you may hear the gruesome story connected with it if you ask around.) Kelly Road winds along the East Fork of the Galena River and goes back under the tracks just before reaching North Ford Road. Turn left and into Council Hill Station, a nice place to stop for a cold apple juice, or whatever.

From the station, ride up North Hill Road to West Council Hill Road and turn left. Follow West Council Hill back through Millbrig Hollow and up, continuing south as it becomes North Council Hill and takes you back into Galena. The farm road that goes off to your left just before you cross the bridge in Millbrig Hollow runs south along the old railroad grade that passes by Tuttle's Mill. This same grade runs north along the river and through the old tunnel in the bluff south of Buncombe Road.

Notes

Miner's Chapel Cemetery   On West Miner, halfway between Northwest and Northeast Miner, you can take a short (0.3 mile) side trip to see one of the old cemeteries in the region—a nice place to rest for a little while.

Stagecoach Trail   Taking West Stagecoach Trail out to Northeast Miner Road would shorten this loop by about 1.8 miles and avoid the unsurfaced section of Buckhill, but I advise you to avoid riding on Stagecoach if you don't have to, because people often drive too fast, and curves and hills hinder visibility. The only reason I ride it is to get on West Guilford Road, which is the only reasonable access to some nice destinations to the east. If you do choose to ride it, be especially alert for traffic.

Ford Road Loop (Galena Cellars Vineyard)

Time: 3 hours   **Distance:** 23.8 miles

Conditions: 5.8 miles unsurfaced; on Buckhill from the bottom of the downhill to the Galena River Valley to West Miner, on Posey Hollow and Kelly over to Ford, a short (0.2 mile) stretch on Ford, and about 1 mile on Northeast Miner between Guilford and Stagecoach. There's a hard climb from the vineyard up to Stagecoach on Ford, and one very steep but quite short section on Northeast Miner before you get to Stagecoach on the return loop. The views from North Ford Road on the return half of the loop are outstanding.

This is an extension of the Posey Hollow/Council Hill Loop. It takes you on a southern instead of northern return loop that includes the Galena Cellars Vineyard Tasting Room on North Ford Road. Through November, on Friday, Saturday, and Sunday, from 11:00 A.M. until dusk, you can stop at the tasting

The tasting room at the Galena Cellars Vineyard

room halfway through this loop and enjoy the view and a glass of wine on the deck, along with local cheese and sausages. To check on changing hours, call 815-777-3330. There is also a two-bedroom rental house on the premises—call 1-800-397-WINE for arrangements. (Scott Lawler, the owner-manager of the winery, and a bicycling enthusiast, said that two of the winners in the Cactus Cup 1994 stayed there while they were in town.)

The Route

To begin, follow the same route as for the Posey Hollow/Council Hill loop, but when you reach North Ford Road, go right instead of left, and follow North Ford to the Galena Cellars Vineyard. From where you hit Ford on the East Fork of the Galena River to the vineyard (about 2 miles), you'll rise about 200 feet, but it's mostly a gradual rise.

After your break, there's some work to do—in the 0.3 mile up to West Stagecoach Trail, you'll climb another 160 feet. There's a reward in store, though, as you cross Stagecoach and continue south on North Ford to West Guilford Road. North Ford runs for a mile on a ridge at about 1100 feet that gives a great view of the countryside, especially south into the panorama of the Galena Territory.

At West Guilford, turn right. It's almost 2 miles to the fork where Guilford bends to the left; go straight there onto Northeast Miner Road (unsurfaced), and follow it up to Stagecoach. Jog right and then left to cross Stagecoach and continue on Northeast Miner. Turn left on West Miner, then turn right on West Buckhill, and follow that back to the junction with North Council Hill and on into Galena the way you came out.

Note

Stagecoach Trail   Although you can see on the map that taking Guilford to Stagecoach and Stagecoach back into Galena would be a shorter return, I don't recommend riding on Stagecoach, where traffic is fast, there is often no shoulder, and curves limit visibility. If you do choose to ride it, stay alert, especially on the downhill S-curve about a mile west of Guilford Road.

New Diggings Loop (New Diggings Store & Inn)

Time: 3 1/4 hours   **Distance:** 26.3 miles

Conditions: All surfaced, except for about 2 miles on North Birkbeck from the Illinois line to West Council Hill. (See the Notes for an alternate route that's all surfaced.)

This is one of the nicest trips around, not only because of the scenery (especially on the loop back), but because of the New Diggings Store & Inn. The best time to plan for is a Sunday afternoon, when there's live music starting around 3:00 P.M. You can enjoy a good rest and have a cold drink before heading back. (You might even want to stay—there are a few rooms, and campsites are available.) Jamie Jones, the owner, plays and sings, and among the folks who come out to make music, some well-known musicians show up every once in a while, including Jim Post, Mick Scott, and Steve Moris.

Coming into New Diggings today, you'd never know that from the 1840s until the early 1900s it was a bustling mining center, first for lead and then for zinc, with a two-story brick school, stores, inns, a pool hall, and a population of around 1400. Up the hill from the New Diggings Store on County I, if you bear left, you can visit the beautiful old St. Augustine church, built in 1844 and designed by Fr. Samuel Mazzuchelli. In the large Masonic Cemetery west of town on County W is the grave of Charles Gear, Hezekiah Gear's brother.

The Route

Take the northeast way out of town, and follow North Council Hill Road all the way to Council Hill (about a half-mile past Bowden Road). Turn left on North Road, and follow it to the junction with County I, at the Illinois/Wisconsin border, where you bear right. Hezekiah Gear worked this region, too, and made another of his big strikes in the area to your left just before the junction. At the bottom of the long downhill on County I, you cross the Kelsey Branch of the Galena River. After the long sweep down and up, you're on a ridge until you cross Ridge Road and start downhill into New Diggings. There's a sign for the old St. Augustine church to your right. You'll find the old Store & Inn at the intersection with County W.

To return, go east on County W for about 3 miles. You'll cross the Galena River and go uphill to the junction with County J, where you bear left and stay on County W, heading downhill. When the road bends sharply to the right after

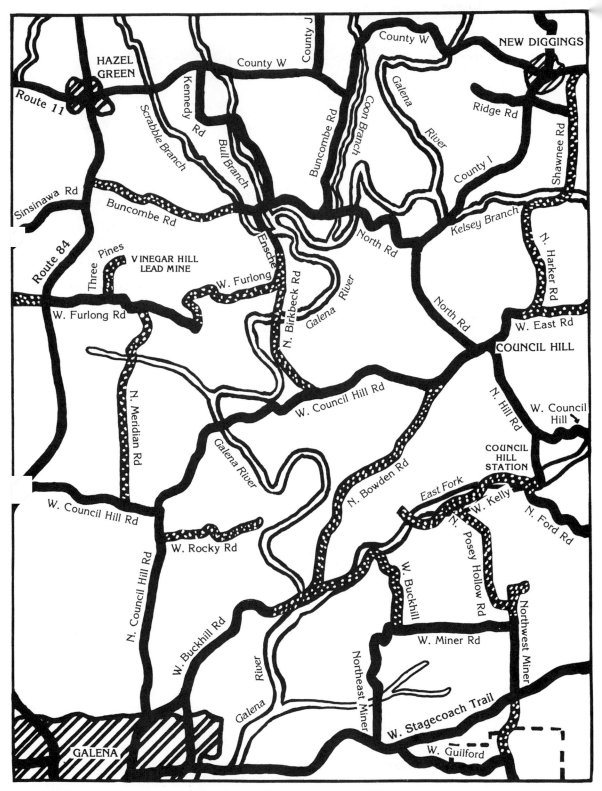

Map 3: New Diggings and Hazel Green

The New Diggings Store & Inn—Jamie (on bike) and Mick Scott

you're on the flat, go straight (leaving County W), and get on Buncombe Road (you'll see a "Rustic Road" sign). Buncombe takes you south along the Coon Branch of the Galena and then (at the junction with North Road) bends right (east) and runs along the Galena River for about a half-mile—a beautiful stretch of road, and one of the few places where you can ride so close to the river.

Just past Kennedy Road (another Rustic Road that runs north to meet County W), you'll find Ensche Road. Turn left there (with the river), and follow it south into Illinois, where it becomes North Birkbeck Road and connects with West Council Hill Road. From the turn onto Ensche, it's about 2.5 miles to West Council Hill, which becomes North Council Hill as it bends south and takes you back into Galena.

Notes

North Road Connection   If you want to skip the unsurfaced section on North Birkbeck and make this ride entirely on surfaced roads, you can use the section of North Road between Buncombe Road and County I. On the return, where Buncombe meets North Road at the Galena River, take a sharp left and follow North Road up to the junction with County I. It's a steep climb, but at least there's a little flat stretch in the middle of it. Continue on North Road back to West Council Hill and turn right, heading southwest and then south back into Galena.

Richardson Road   Richardson Road (not shown on Map 3) goes off to your left as you're coming down from North Road on County I. This is a dead-end road that leads into the Richardson farm—give them their privacy, unless you have some kind of emergency.

Scales Mound Loop

Time: 3 3/4 hours   **Distance:** 30 miles

Conditions: 3.4 miles unsurfaced, on West East Road from about North Harker Road to North Culvert Road and for about a mile after turning south on North Culvert, with another 0.7-mile stretch on West Culvert from the sharp left bend to Jewell Lane.

This is a long, but very beautiful ride that gives you a chance for rest and refreshment in the little town of Scales Mound, just east and north of the geological Scales Mound, and just southwest of Charles Mound, the highest point in Illinois (currently private property, but on the market). An early settler named Scales owned the mound, and gave it and the town his name. Scales Mound is 15.4 miles from Galena, and you can plan to get there for lunch (or breakfast, if you like to ride early), stopping at Friends, Inc. (closed Sunday) just north of the railroad tracks as you come into town, or at the Unique Country Inn, just south of the tracks.

Scales Mound was a main stop on the Frink & Walker Stage Line (the return route on West Council Hill follows the old trail). When the Illinois Central came through in 1854 and put Frink & Walker out of business, it became a railroad town. The railroaders changed shifts at Scales Mound, and there was a big Y for switching. It's a quiet and friendly town today. The spirit of the place and its people has been caught in the photographs and text of *Neighbors*, a book by Archie Lieberman that you might enjoy taking a look at.

The visual high point is on the return, as you ride on West Council Hill Road across the western shoulder of Scales Mound. From there, on a clear day, you can see Sinsinawa Mound to the east, and even the bluffs on the Iowa side of the Mississippi River.

Looking west from the base of Scales Mound

The Route

Take the northeast route out of Galena, and follow North and West Council Hill Roads all the way out to and through Council Hill. Where the main road bends right (becoming North Hill Road and heading down to Council Hill Station), keep going straight, passing the Council Hill Cemetery, and you'll be on West East Road, which becomes unsurfaced around where North Harker Road (all unsurfaced) takes off north to your left, running up to County W and New Diggings.

Stay on West East to the stop sign, and then turn right on North Culvert Road. After about a mile and a half, you'll see where this road gets its name, as you go under the tracks and then cross the East Fork of the Galena River. At the sharp bend to the left, North Culvert becomes West Culvert, and there's a short unsurfaced section, ending at the stop sign at Jewell Lane. West Culvert brings you right into the town of Scales Mound after about 2 miles. To your left, you

The culvert on North Culvert Road

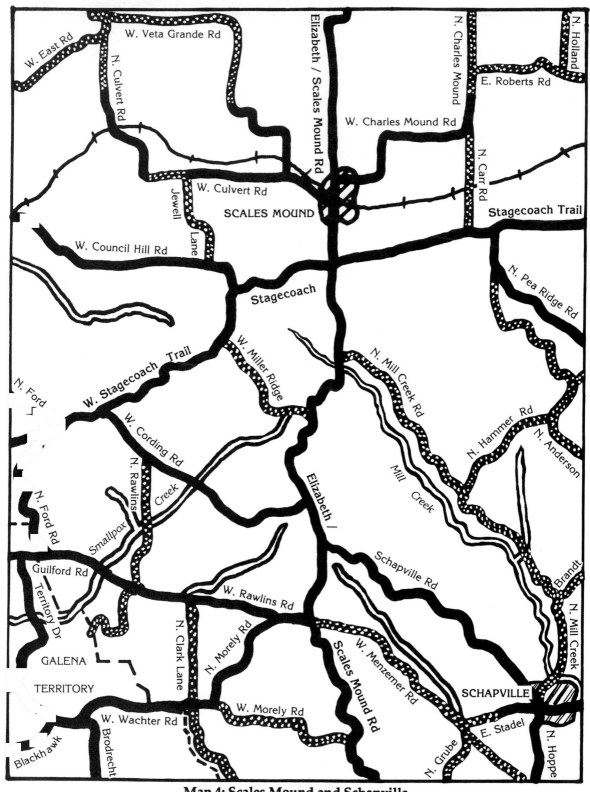

Map 4: Scales Mound and Schapville

see the gently rounded rise of Charles Mound—not a dramatic topographic feature, but still the highest point in Illinois.

To return, go south on Elizabeth/Scales Mound Road to West Stagecoach Trail, and turn right. In the stagecoach days, there was a flourishing blacksmith shop at this junction. Although I don't ordinarily advise riding on Stagecoach, the section from here to West Council Hill has a pretty good shoulder and no sharp curves or steep hills. Still, traffic is fast—stay alert as you ride the mile to where you bend right to get on West Council Hill Road (just past the big "Jesus Saves" rock).

West Council Hill takes you north along the west side of Scales Mound, and then bends west and runs gradually downhill for about 3 miles back to the East Fork of the Galena River. Then there's about a mile of up and down before you get to North Hill Road, where you turn right and go up to West Council Hill, bending left. For variety on the way back, go off to your left on North Bowden Road, and follow it down to Buckhill, where you turn right and head back to the junction with North Council Hill and on into Galena.

East

Introduction

There is some very beautiful country to ride through in the area east of Galena, though it's not rich in "destinations" or in mining history. The Galena Territory offers some wonderful views and a look at some luxurious homes and condos, as well as all services for food and drink. For the feeling of being "out in the country," however, you will prefer the ride out to Schapville.

Refer to Maps 2 and 4 in the preceding section for the routes described here. The maps in this book don't show much detail about the Galena Territory because the road system is too complex, and a good, detailed map is available out there. From that map, you can plan numerous options for loops within the Territory.

The safest bicycle access to the region (see Map 2) is to take the northeast route out of Galena, follow Buckhill to West Miner, and then go south on Northwest Miner to Stagecoach Trail. Turn left and then right on West Guilford, from which you can go into the Territory on Thunder Bay Road (which takes you past the falls at the outlet of Lake Galena) or on Territory Drive (which takes you by the marina at the other end of the lake).

Since this is such a roundabout way to get onto West Guilford road, however, I would say that to save your time and energy for exploring new territory, it's better to heed the advice in the Portage notes for these routes, and carry your bike by car out to the Eagle Ridge Inn & Resort (unless you're staying out there already), and ride from there. If you're determined to bike all the way and choose to shorten the trip, ride out Stagecoach Trail from Galena to West Guilford (see the route description below), being very watchful of the traffic.

The Galena Territory Loop

Time: 2 1/2 hours (to Eagle Ridge Inn and back only)

Distance: 19.2 miles (round trip to Eagle Ridge Inn and back)

Conditions: All surfaced

If you are interested in riding out to see the Eagle Ridge Inn & Resort, and the homes and golf courses of the Galena Territory, plan on a morning ride out to the Inn (about 1 1/4 hours) and a little breakfast once you get there. You can eat at the Inn, or get food at the General Store and Bakery (or bring your own and find a nice spot overlooking Lake Galena).

At the main desk or at the bicycle-rental area, you can get the Resort Facilities Map and plan whatever kind of route you'd like on the many roads within the Territory. There are also some bicycle paths shown on the map, mostly closer to the resort core. You can be back to the resort area for lunch and a rest before riding back into Galena.

The Route

The only efficient way to ride out to the Galena Territory is to use Stagecoach Trail. There's a steep climb through an S-curve just after Heller Lane where you should be especially alert for traffic; get over onto the gravel shoulder when you hear traffic coming. It's 4 miles from the river intersection to West Guilford Road, where you turn right. Guilford bends right at the bottom of a long downhill (where Northeast Miner Road goes up to the left). Follow Guilford to Territory Drive, and turn right, heading into the heart of the Territory.

Territory Drive takes you for a long downhill into the hollow of Smallpox Creek, which fills Lake Galena, and then into a long uphill workout to the Owners'

The falls on Thunder Bay Road in the Galena Territory

Club. Follow Territory Drive to the stop sign at West Wachter Drive, and turn right. Follow Wachter to where it tees into Eagle Ridge Drive; you'll see the main resort complex to your right, and the General Store and Bakery on your left.

You could also turn right onto Thunder Bay Road, just south of the junction with Northeast Miner, and follow it around south and west to Eagle Ridge Drive. Turning left there will bring you to Eagle Ridge Inn. Just before the junction with Mt. Hope Road, you'll probably want to stop and enjoy the waterfall at the western end of Lake Galena, which feeds Smallpox Creek. If you came out on Territory Drive, loop back to Guilford on Thunder Bay, and vice versa.

Portage

To save your energy for riding around in the Territory itself, and to be as safe as possible by avoiding the ride on Stagecoach, you can take your bike out to the Inn by car, and skip the trip from Galena (assuming you're not already staying at Eagle Ridge). It's 6.8 miles from Galena to Territory Drive, so driving out with your bike saves 13.6 miles of riding. Since it gives you the greatest amount of time at your destination, I'd say driving out is best—though the ride out on West Guilford between Stagecoach and Territory Drive is a nice one. If you do want to ride Stagecoach, the best time to do it is in the early morning when traffic is lightest.

Note

Heller Lane   Heller Lane is a dead-end, unsurfaced road that is pleasant but not worth a special effort if you're on a longer trip. I sometimes ride out there and back in the early morning, when traffic is light on Stage-coach, for some exercise to start the day. If you go out that way, be ready for the dogs at the first farm on the left.

Schapville Loop

Time: 3 1/2 hours   **Distance:** 28.2 miles

Conditions: 3.1 miles unsurfaced (all on the return route described); 0.9 mile on East Stadel Road and 2.2 miles on West Menzemer Road. There's a long, hard climb on West Rawlins on your way up to Elizabeth/Scales Mound Road, and then the road stays generally level on a high ridge as you ride north and then southeast and finally down into Schapville. The loop back leads up through a hollow that roughly parallels the high road you came in on, and then rises to meet Elizabeth/Scales Mound Road at West Rawlins.

Schapville is a very small community with two old country churches and no services, though by the time this book is published there may be a little general store open there—look for it on your right as you go through town.

The Route

To get to Schapville, go out West Stagecoach to West Guilford (see the description for the Galena Territory). Go on past Territory Drive and continue across Smallpox Creek and through Guilford. West Guilford becomes West Rawlins Road at the junction with North Rawlins Road. General Rawlins was one of the nine Civil War generals from the Galena area, and you'll ride by his house about 0.3 mile past North Clark Lane, on your right.

The country home of General Rawlins on West Rawlins Road

Just after the Rawlins house comes the long uphill workout to the ridge that carries Elizabeth/Scales Mound Road. Bear left at the junction with North Morley to stay on West Rawlins, and you'll soon reach Elizabeth/Scales Mound. Turn left there, and ride north about a mile, staying alert for fast traffic, to West Schapville Road, where you turn right. West Schapville runs southeast along a ridge and then down into Schapville. You'll see the first church on your right coming into town. The other church is at the other end of town on your left, on the way down to Mill Creek.

For variety on the return, leave Schapville on East Stadel Road, and bear right at the junction with West Menzemer Road, which rises gradually through a hollow leading back up to Elizabeth/Scales Mound Road, just 0.1 mile south of West Rawlins. The scenery along West Menzemer is outstanding as the road rises. Go right and then left, and you're back on West Rawlins, heading back to Galena the way you came out.

Farmhouse and valley view from West Menzemer Road

Note

West Morley Road   On the return, if you'd like some beautiful valley scenery and a good workout, go left on Elizabeth/Scales Mound from West Menzemer, instead of right to West Rawlins, and ride south (stay alert) to West Morley, an unsurfaced road. Turn right on West Morley, and you'll drop steeply into Snipe Hollow, which opens out to the south. Running west for 1.7 miles, the road falls and rises three times and meets North Clark Lane, where it becomes West Wachter and takes you back to the Inn.

Portage

To shorten this loop and avoid the ride on Stagecoach, you can take your bike by car to the Eagle Ridge Inn & Resort at the Galena Territory and start out from there. If you want to explore there as well, you can get a Resort Facilities Map at the front desk that shows all the roads in the Territory. To ride from the Inn to Schapville, take West Wachter Road west, and just past the intersection with North Clark Lane, go left on North Morley Road (mistakenly called Murray Road on the resort map). North Morley is surfaced and follows a ridge to West Rawlins, where you bear right and continue as described above.

South, Southeast

Introduction

Some of the most scenic country around Galena lies to the south and southeast. Snipe Hollow, Long Hollow, Irish Hollow, and access to the Mississippi River all lie in this area, and riding through it makes it easy to understand why the Indians of this region, who called it Manitoumi Land, believed these hills and valleys were the special preserve of their Great Spirit.

This area is also rich in mining history. Chestnut Mountain Resort is in the heart of what was known as the New California Diggings along the bluffs north and south of the ski lifts. The openings of some horizontal mines dug into the bluffs are still visible from South River Road, though many are being sealed. Blackjack Road is named for the old Marsden-Blackjack Mine; its remains are still visible along the west side of the road just north of Hart John Road. About a mile and a half further down Blackjack, on your left heading south, you can still see a scar on the hillside where about 7 acres caved in at the Bautsch mine.

Speaking of Blackjack Road, I'll note here (and repeat later) that this is a dangerous road. You have to ride it to get access to Irish Hollow and Pilot Knob, but it's best to stay off of it when you can between Galena and Chestnut Mountain. There are hills and curves and lots of people who drive too fast. South of there, however, between Chestnut and Hanover, there is not so much traffic, and the road stays up on a ridge, so visibility is better. Though the routes I describe tend to avoid it, the views from this section are outstanding; just be cautious about traffic if you choose to include it in a route you plan.

Irish Hollow/Rocky Hill Loop

Time: 1 1/2 hours   **Distance:** 12.1 miles

Conditions: All surfaced roads, except for 1 mile between Irish Hollow and Rocky Hill, but watch for patches of loose gravel, especially on Rocky Hill.

South Irish Hollow Road leads through one of the most beautiful areas southeast of Galena, and the view from West Cemetery Road, looking north to Horseshoe Mound and Dygert's Mound, is well worth the challenging climb that leads up to it. Take a break from the saddle and enjoy it.

Dygert's Mound and Horseshoe Mound seen from Cemetery Road

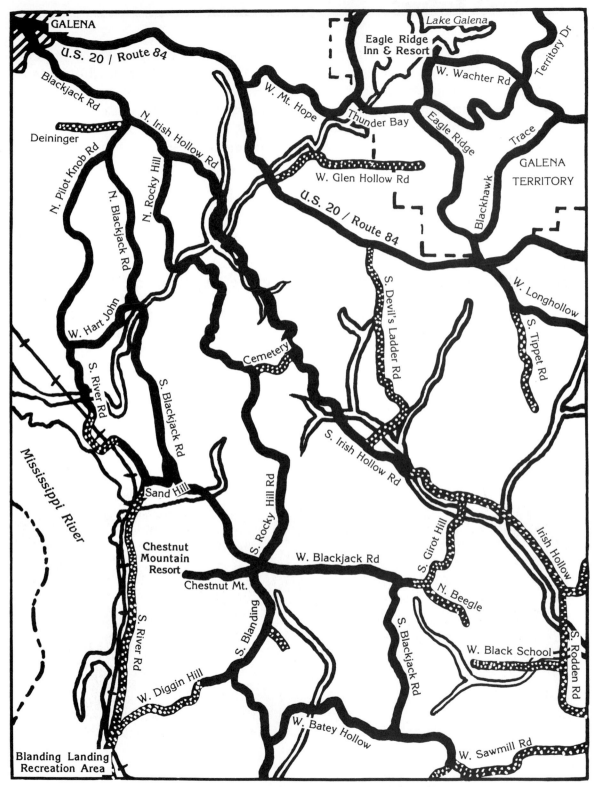

Map 5: Chestnut Mountain, Blanding, Irish Hollow

The buildings at the Fried Green Tomatoes restaurant complex stood in ruins for years before being extensively renovated. This was the old County Poor Farm and Asylum. Originally built in 1850, it was destroyed by fire in January of 1870. The buildings there now date from the reconstruction in the early 1870s. Additional renovation is currently under way to provide a 32-room inn. The food at Fried Green Tomatoes is excellent, and casual clothes are fine, except for cut-offs and tank tops.

The Route

Leave Galena by the southeast route, and follow Blackjack Road. At the top of the hill going up to Dygert's Mound, you'll come to the intersection with North Irish Hollow Road (look for the Fried Green Tomatoes sign), where you go left. Ahead and to your right is Hangman's Hill, where 2,000 people once gathered to see a hanging. Just beyond Fried Green Tomatoes, bear left on South Irish Hollow.

Prospect Hill Cemetery, at Rocky Hill and Cemetery Roads

Towards the bottom of the first downhill stretch, on your right, was the site of the old Bower Mine, infamous for its problems with water. Not far past there, you'll cross Smallpox Creek. After the difficult uphill past the farm with the pond, turn right on West Cemetery Road (unsurfaced), and follow that to Rocky Hill Road. If you stop to enjoy a walk around Prospect Hill Cemetery, you may find the grave of a Scandinavian worker killed during the construction of the half-mile-long Winston Tunnel, which runs under Rocky Hill Road further south. The inscription says he's buried at the west end of the tunnel.

Turn right, and head back north on Rocky Hill. Take it easy on the steep downhill stretch, which has some sharp curves and plenty of loose gravel. About a mile north of that steep hill, the road goes down again to cross Smallpox Creek. Once you climb up from the creek valley, the road stays almost level, rising slightly to the junction with North Irish Hollow. Bear left to Blackjack, and turn right to head back into Galena.

South Girot Hill Loop (Chestnut Mountain Resort)

Time: 2 1/2 hours   **Distance:** 19.2 miles

Conditions: 2.3 miles unsurfaced, starting on South Irish Hollow about a mile before South Girot Hill Road, which is all unsurfaced.

This is an especially nice ride, not only because of the scenery farther along South Irish Hollow, and the shady seclusion of South Girot Hill Road, but because it offers the option of stopping at about the halfway point at Chestnut Mountain Lodge. You can rest, look out over the Mississippi, eat if you like (breakfast starts at 7:00 A.M., seven days a week), and go on your way. Here, too, there are some off-road bike trails—inquire at the Lodge.

The Route

This ride is an extended version of the Irish Hollow/Rocky Hill Loop already described. Follow that route as far as West Cemetery Road, but then continue on South Irish Hollow Road. Once you reach the flat bottom of Irish Hollow, it's about 0.7 mile to South Girot Hill Road, which goes up to the right. Turning on to it, you cross a creek and then the old Chicago & Northwestern railroad bed, which bends northwest toward the east end of the Winston Tunnel (now closed off). Both ends of the tunnel are on private property.

The Mississippi from the Chestnut Mountain ski lift

South Girot Hill rises, mostly gradually, for about 1.3 miles to meet Blackjack Road, where you turn right. From there it's about 1.6 miles along the ridge to the intersection with South Blanding Road and South Rocky Hill Road. You'll see the Chestnut Mountain sign. To get to the resort, turn left and then right on Chestnut Mountain Road—it's a nice break.

Return to Galena by going back out to Blackjack and across it onto South Rocky Hill Road. About 0.9 mile from that intersection, you're riding right over the Winston Tunnel, which cuts through the ridge about 160 feet under the road. Follow Rocky Hill back to Blackjack and on into town.

Notes

Devil's Ladder Road   About a mile and a half past West Cemetery Hill, just after the farm at 1813 South Irish Hollow, the narrow, unmarked gravel road that goes off across the hollow to your left is Devil's Ladder Road, a real rollercoaster that connects with Highway 20 about 2 miles west of (downhill from) the entrance to the Galena Territory. You might want to explore this road a little—it's secluded and runs mostly through woods after you cross the hollow— but I wouldn't recommend traveling its length unless you're in really good shape. Some stretches are extremely steep (at least a 20% grade). It's 2.6 miles to the highway, and then there you are with all that traffic going by at 60+ mph, so it's turn around and do it again the other way (unless you've arranged for a car to meet you). I don't recommend going anywhere from there except back the way you came.

The Wooded Wonderland campground is off Devil's Ladder, about 0.8 mile south of Highway 20. It's a very rustic place with 100 campsites on 300 acres ($4.00 per person; 815-777-1223).

West Beegle Road   West Beegle goes off to your left as you get up on the ridge near the end of South Girot Hill. It dead-ends into private property after running a short way through land owned by the State of Illinois.

Blanding Loop

Time: 3 hours   **Distance:** 23.6 miles

Conditions: Approx. 6.6 miles unsurfaced on the main route described.

The route described is a beautiful and challenging ride that brings you right down by the Mississippi. Along the way is a riverside recreation area with campsites ($7.00 a night; someone is there for registration between 7:00 P.M. and 10:00 P.M.), and at Blanding you can get food and drink at Blanding Tavern seven days a week. Many variations are possible in the route I will describe. Several roads go through the region southeast of Galena (see Maps 5 and 6, and the Alternative Routes), but I'll suggest what I think is the safest and most scenic ride.

The return route leads along the base of the bluffs south and north of Chestnut that were known as the California Diggings, and gives you a chance to get close to the Mississippi.

The Route

Take the southeast route out of Galena, and follow Blackjack Road. At the top of the hill going up to Dygert's Mound (on your right), you'll come to the intersection with North Irish Hollow Road (there's a Fried Green Tomatoes sign). Go left onto Irish Hollow, follow it past the restaurant, and then bear left to get on South Irish Hollow. After the difficult uphill, going up past the farm with the pond, turn right on West Cemetery Road (unsurfaced), and follow that to Rocky Hill Road. Turn left, and you'll have a beautiful ride along the ridge to where Rocky Hill ends at Blackjack, right across from the road into Chestnut Mountain Inn and Resort.

(I don't recommend going out on Rocky Hill, because traffic is a little heavier, and you may not have good control of your bike on the long, difficult uphill. If you decide to go out that way, stay alert for traffic on the uphill, and walk your bike if you're really struggling.)

Cross Blackjack, and head south on South Blanding Road. (If you want to look over the facilities and the view at Chestnut Mountain, and maybe stop to rest or eat, take the right turn that leads to the resort.) After about a mile and a half on South Blanding, turn right on West Diggin Hill Road, an unmarked, unsurfaced road (it has a stop sign at Blanding Road). You'll stay on a ridge for about a mile, and then Diggin Hill bears left and into a long, steep downhill along a heavily wooded ravine. This is one of my favorite stretches in the region. I rode it uphill the first time—it's more fun going down. Take it slowly; make it last, and watch for wildlife.

Diggin Hill ends at South River Road, the route you'll take back to Galena. Bear left now, continuing south, and be alert for the sharp right through the railroad underpass just after you get onto River Road. Not quite a mile down the road, you'll come to Blanding Landing Recreation Area, a nice place to stop and eat if you've brought a picnic.

Another 1.2 miles along the river brings you to Blanding and a chance to stretch and have a cold drink and some food at Blanding Tavern. You'll probably meet some people and share some stories.

To return to Galena, go back north on South River Road. A little over a mile north of where Diggin Hill meets River Road, there's a very steep downhill with thick dust and gravel that's half washed out by rain. It's safest to walk it through the steepest part. Up the creek valley that goes off to your right after that steep

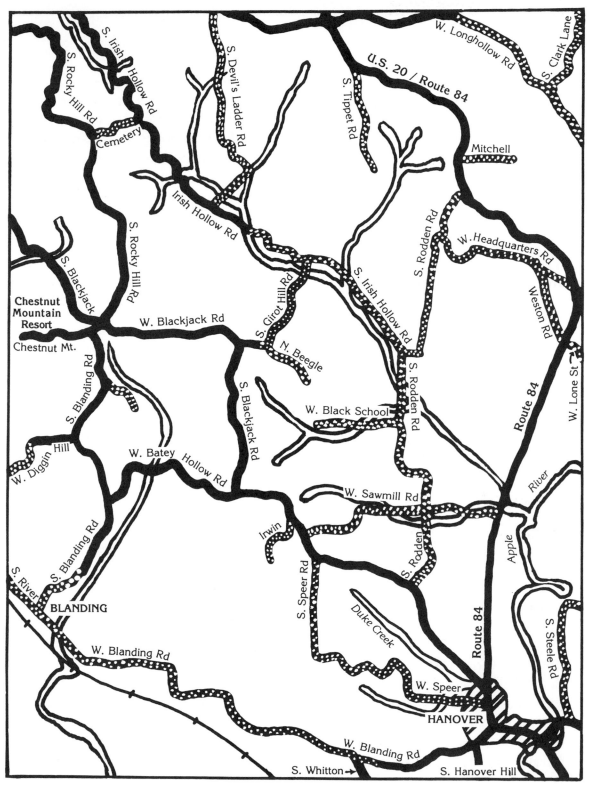

Map 6: Blanding, Irish Hollow, Hanover

little hill was the old Royal Princess Mine. A little farther and you're at the bottom of the Chestnut Mountain ski runs.

Riding on, you'll pass Sand Hill Road going off to the right, cross and recross the railroad tracks, and start heading gradually uphill. When you pass West Hart John Road going off to your right, you'll be on South Pilot Knob Road, which rises steadily and takes you over the east shoulder of Pilot Knob (a landmark for riverboat pilots looking for the mouth of the Galena River, where a signal fire was sometimes built at night). Now you're on North Pilot Knob and heading northeast back to Blackjack Road, where you turn left to go back into town.

Alternative Routes

Pilot Knob   Of course, the least demanding route, which avoids the strenuous uphill on South Irish Hollow, is to both go and return by what I've described as the return. Just ride past Irish Hollow on your way out Blackjack, and continue a short way to Pilot Knob Road. Turn right, and follow on. You do have to climb the shoulder of Pilot Knob, but that's not so bad compared to the main uphill on Irish Hollow, and then it's downhill to the Mississippi and mostly level to Blanding.

South Blanding   For another alternative, go out on Pilot Knob and South River Road, and return on South Blanding Road to Chestnut, a 3.5-mile stretch that's unsurfaced for the first mile and runs through a deeply wooded area after the rise to the ridge. Take Rocky Hill (and then maybe Irish Hollow) back to Galena. Remember to keep a sharp eye on traffic if you choose to return on Blackjack (which I don't advise).

Sand Hill   If you want a look at some of the easily visible old mining sites, you can stay on Blackjack instead of going left on Irish Hollow or right on Pilot Knob, although the safest way to do this is by car. If you're going to ride, stay especially alert for traffic. Follow Blackjack out past Hart John Road to Sand Hill Road, and turn right. (You could also go right on Hart John, which takes you over to South Pilot Knob just before it becomes South River Road.) Sand Hill will take you to South River Road, and you can ride that along the river all the way to Blanding. If you're driving, don't go south on South River—you can't get a car over it south of Chestnut. Instead, turn right, and loop back to Blackjack on Pilot Knob.

If you choose this way, and would rather not go back over so much of what you've already traveled, you might prefer to ride back from Blanding by taking South Blanding Road back up to Chestnut and Blackjack. From there, it's safest to take Rocky Hill (and then perhaps Irish Hollow) back toward Galena. Use your brakes and take it easy on the steep downhills; there's usually a lot of loose gravel on the curves.

Note

Blackjack　　I don't recommend riding all the way out to Chestnut on Blackjack Road. The traffic is often heavy and fast, and it's safest to avoid the long, steep uphill in those conditions. You will have seen the best of the scenery on Blackjack between Galena and Chestnut by the time you turn off on Sand Hill.

Hanover Loop

Time: 4 hours　　　**Distance:** 32 miles

Conditions: 14.4 miles unsurfaced on the route described (see Alternatives); 4.9 miles on South Irish Hollow and South Rodden to Blackjack, and 9.5 miles on West Blanding and South River Road returning. Roughly 4 miles of the ride down are over mostly level country on South Irish Hollow and South Rodden. On the return, about 8 miles are over mostly level roads through bottomlands of the Mississippi and along the river.

This is an extension of the Blanding Loop that gives you a chance to eat, rest, and look around in the little town of Hanover on the Apple River, home of the world's largest mallard duck hatchery, Whistling Wings. A variety of alternative routes are possible, as you can see from Maps 5, 6, and 7. The ride down through Irish Hollow and the ride back along the river take you through the whole spectrum of scenic possibilities. In the days before the damming of the Mississippi, the river was not as wide, and there was much more land on the river side of South River Road. The area was known as Sand Prairie, and much of it was farmed.

The Route

Follow the same route as for the South Girot Hill Loop, but continue south on South Irish Hollow Road instead of turning right at Girot Hill. Bear right, continuing south, at the junction with South Rodden Road. The road becomes more rolling, and after the stop sign at the intersection with West Sawmill Road, it rises into what becomes a steep, half-mile climb to the ridge that carries South Blackjack Road, about 240 feet higher than Sawmill. Turn left on Blackjack, and follow it downhill into Hanover, at the junction with Illinois Route 84. The main part of town is to your right, across the Apple River.

To return, assuming you've crossed the river, go back north across the bridge and take an immediate left on Fulton, which bends south to follow the river. At the junction with South Hanover Hill Road, Fulton becomes West Blanding Road. Bear right to stay on it, and look for some uphill work before you coast down to the bottomland. After that, you'll have a generally level ride through Blanding and all the way back up the Mississippi River, until you have to climb up toward Pilot Knob. West Blanding becomes South River Road as you come through Blanding. (South Blanding goes off to your right and up to Blackjack at Chestnut Mountain.)

Follow South River Road up the river past Chestnut and Sand Hill and on past West Hart John Road, where it becomes South Pilot Knob Road. Continue up the east side of Pilot Knob and on to Blackjack, where you turn left and head back into Galena.

Alternative Routes

West Sawmill / Speer Road   This variation adds 2.9 miles to the trip down to Hanover, all unsurfaced except for a short stretch on South Blackjack, but it also adds some of the most beautiful views in the region as you ride along Speer Road. Turn right at the stop sign at West Sawmill Road, and ride west up to South Blackjack Road. It's a harder climb than on South Rodden—there's a section of 15% grade where the road rises 160 feet in 0.3 mile. It's a beautiful stretch of road, though, and runs by a farm that raises Charolais cattle—creamy white and beautiful to see.

Go left on Blackjack and then right on South Speer Road. The view is outstanding both east and west from this ridge, and then you bend sharply to the east and get a wonderful view of Hanover as you drop down toward the town.

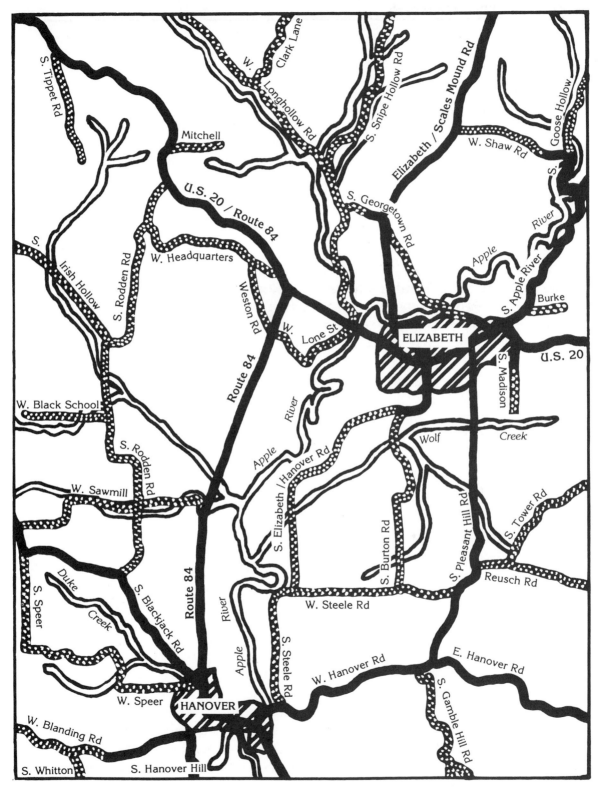

Map 7: Hanover, Elizabeth, Long Hollow

The village of Hanover from West Speer Road

South Blanding to Blackjack   On the return trip, if you'd rather not ride the gravel all the way back up along the river, you can ride out of Hanover to Blanding, but then take South Blanding Road (which becomes surfaced after about a mile) to the right and up to Blackjack at Chestnut Mountain. From there, to avoid riding Blackjack between Chestnut and Galena, take the Rocky Hill route back to Galena.

Notes

West Batey Hollow Road   West Batey Hollow Road is another very beautiful road that connects South Blackjack and South Blanding. Recently surfaced (watch for lots of loose gravel), it runs through the hollow that opens out to Blanding, connecting with South Blanding Road after about 1.4 miles. The difference in elevation between Blackjack and the creek that runs through Batey Hollow is 240 feet, and at the steepest part of the downhill from Blackjack, you lose 140 feet in 0.3 mile—another road that it's nicer to ride down than up. There are several ways to work it into one of the routes described in this region, and I highly recommend it.

South Rodden Road   Between South Irish Hollow and Highway 20, South Rodden Road is all unsurfaced and rises about 300 feet to the ridge that carries the highway. Most of the rise (200 feet) is over the first 0.7 mile from Irish Hollow. It's about 2.2 miles to the highway. If you have the energy for the climb, it would make a good scenic detour to ride up to the highway and back. (I don't advise going anywhere on Highway 20 once you get up there.)

West Headquarters Road   If you're looking for a challenge, West Headquarters Road (unsurfaced) offers almost as much difficulty as Devil's Ladder Road. At its west end, as it meets South Rodden Road, is a 13% grade; the road rises (or falls, if you're heading east) 200 feet in 0.3 mile. It's up and down all the way to where it meets Weston, and then levels out and ends at Highway 20. Weston Road runs downhill southeast to Route 84, and just across the road is West Lone Street, which circles north to Highway 20. This area was the center of the lead mining industry around Elizabeth. Just across the highway from where Lone Street comes out, you'll see the southern end of Longhollow Road.

Headquarters, Weston, and Lone thus make a connection between Irish Hollow and Longhollow that avoids major roads (see Map 7). You could plan a route to Elizabeth using this connection—going up Longhollow to South Georgetown, and then back down into Elizabeth.

Elizabeth Loop

Time: 4 3/4 hours   **Distance:** 37.9 miles

Conditions: 9.6 miles unsurfaced; 1.1 on North Clark, 1.7 on West Morley, 5.4 on Snipe Hollow, Longhollow, and South Georgetown, and 1.4 on South Goose Hollow. The most serious work is on North Clark as it rises from West Rawlins; on West Morley, which falls and rises three times as it crosses the top of Snipe Hollow; and on the last part of South Goose Hollow and East Hoffman up to Elizabeth/Scales Mound Road.

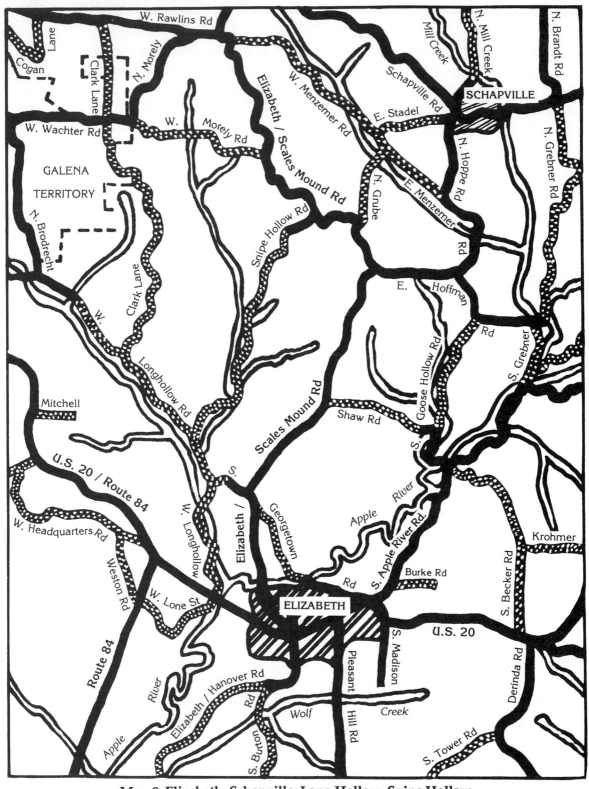

Map 8: Elizabeth, Schapville, Long Hollow, Snipe Hollow

This is a long and challenging ride that takes you through the most beautiful and least-traveled parts of the countryside in this area. You can plan easier and shorter loops to Elizabeth, but this route is probably the most rewarding. The nicest scenery on the way down is on North Clark, West Morley, and Snipe Hollow. Elizabeth is a pleasant resting place. You can find food and drink, and you'll probably enjoy a visit to Bishop's general store. South Goose Hollow and East Hoffman on the way back are also very scenic.

If funding comes through, the town of Elizabeth plans to reconstruct a replica of the old Apple River Fort that stood on the hillside east of town. Check it out in 1996.

The Route

To get to Elizabeth, start by following the route described for the Schapville Loop (see the preceding section), but when you come to North Clark Lane as you're riding east on Rawlins, turn right. North Clark follows a creek at first, and then rises along the side of a ridge. After about a mile, there's a stop sign where West Wachter Road comes in from the west, and becomes West Morley at the intersection. Turn left, and head east on West Morley. Just past North Morley, which goes off to your left, West Morley drops steeply, losing around 240 feet in 0.3 mile, takes you across the valley at the top of Snipe Hollow, which opens out to the south, and then climbs back up to meet Elizabeth/Scales Mound Road, where you turn right.

Look for North Snipe Hollow Road about a mile south (see Map 8), and turn right again. You'll ride through woods along a ridge for about half a mile and then start the long and relatively gradual descent into Snipe Hollow. Bear left as you merge with West Longhollow Road. As the road bends left (east), you'll come to a fork, where you bear left to get on South Georgetown Road. (Long- hollow goes off to your right, continuing south to meet the Apple River and Highway 20.)

Bear right onto Elizabeth/Scales Mound Road as you meet it, and then left to get back onto South Georgetown after about 0.2 mile. Georgetown Road, by the way, follows one of the oldest stagecoach trails in the area, which used to lead up to Flint Hills Pass. You'll ride down to cross the Apple River on a fine old iron bridge, and then up into Elizabeth, meeting Highway 20 as it goes through town.

The beginning of the descent into Snipe Hollow

To return, go left at the other end of town on South Apple River Road. About 2 miles northeast of Elizabeth, turn left across the river onto South Goose Hollow Road, which is surfaced as far as Shaw Road. Follow Goose Hollow all the way up to where it meets East Hoffman Road, and bear left on East Hoffman, heading northeast. Bear left again to stay on East Hoffman heading west and up to Elizabeth/Scales Mound Road. (If you're an iron bridge fanatic, you might want to stay on Apple River Road to where it meets South Grebner. Bear left and follow Grebner up to the junction with East Hoffman. To your right on North Grebner is an iron bridge over Hell's Branch of the Apple River. Go left on Hoffman, though, to get back on the route described—see Map 8.)

Turn right and follow Elizabeth/Scales Mound for about 3 miles (stay alert for fast traffic) to West Rawlins Road, and turn left. You'll pass North Morley and then head into a great downhill (see the cover photo) that levels out at North Clark. Continue back into Galena the way you came out.

The iron bridge over the Apple River on Georgetown Road

Alternative Route

For a shorter and easier loop to Elizabeth, stay on Clark Lane instead of turning on West Morley. South Clark (all unsurfaced) stays high along a ridge, and then descends into Long Hollow, about a mile and a half above where it joins Snipe Hollow. Turn left onto Longhollow Road, and follow it southeast to South Georgetown Road and on into Elizabeth as described above.

To return, go back the way you came, but for some change of scene, stay on Longhollow past where South Clark Lane comes into it, continuing to the northwest until you reach North Brodrecht Road. Turn right there, and enjoy a rest stop at Shenandoah Stable in the Galena Territory. Continue north on Brodrecht to West Wachter, and turn right, heading east to North Clark Lane, where you turn left and ride back to Galena as you came out.

Portage

Once again, to shorten this loop and avoid the ride on Stagecoach, you can take your bike by car to the Eagle Ridge Inn & Resort at the Galena Territory and start out from there. You can get a Resort Facilities Map at the front desk that shows all the roads in the Territory if you want to explore there as well. To ride from the Inn to Elizabeth, take West Wachter Road west to the intersection with North Clark Lane, and choose either the longer or shorter of the loops described above (or plan another of your own).

Note

Shaw Road   Shaw Road, which connects South Goose Hollow and Elizabeth/Scales Mound Road, is unsurfaced except for the section where it rises about 140 feet in a little over 0.2 mile, just west of Goose Hollow. After that climb, it stays fairly level until it rises another 100 feet, more gradually, as it approaches Elizabeth/Scales Mound Road.

ORDER FORM

If you would like to order additional copies of this book, please fill in the information below, and mail this page with your check or money order to

Omnivore Press/NMES

706 Park Avenue

Galena, IL 61036

Please send me_____**copies of** *Bicycling Around Galena* **at $8.95 per copy.**

Total: _____

Illinois residents please add 6.25% sales tax.   Tax: _____

Shipping and handling: $3.00_____

Total amount enclosed: _____

Name_____

Address_____

City_____

State_____Zip_____

If you have any comments or suggestions for improving an updated edition, please send them along. Thank you.